getting the word out

A HANDBOOK FOR READERS

Christopher George Hoyer

Augsburg Fortress

GETTING THE WORD OUT
A Handbook for Readers

Also available:
Leading Worship Matters: A Sourcebook for Preparing Worship Leaders
    (ISBN 978-1-4514-7806-8)
Serving the Assembly's Worship: A Handbook for Assisting Ministers (ISBN 978-1-4514-7808-2)
Altar Guild and Sacristy Handbook, 4th rev. ed. (ISBN 978-1-4514-7809-9)
Worship Matters: An Introduction to Worship (Participant book ISBN 978-1-4514-3605-1;
    Leader guide ISBN 978-1-4514-3604-4)

Cover design: Laurie Ingram
Cover photo: Mark Christianson
Interior design: Ivy Palmer Skrade
Editor: Suzanne Burke

Manufactured in the U.S.A.

ISBN 978-1-4514-7807-5

17   16   15   14   13   1   2   3   4   5

Contents

"

Dare to speak the
word with greater
boldness and without fear.
Philippians 1:14b

A wonderful word of
encouragement from blessed
St. Paul to every reader.

Introduction

In an e-mail to her pastor, a parishioner wrote concerning her four-year-old: "Libby asked yesterday when Jesus was going to come down and see her since he is just up there and not talking! I can't keep up with her."

It is the challenge and the joy of those who read in the assembly to dispel this child's commonly held misconception. Let there be no doubt that at the announcement of the reading, "A reading from . . . ," Jesus comes down. Let there be no doubt that with each reading from the scripture Jesus is talking. We underscore that reality at the conclusion of each reading when we declare this to be "the word of the Lord."

How shall we rediscover and experience this truth? That is the task of this little handbook for readers.

The frightening and holy truth of the matter is that God deigns to use human beings to vocalize God's truth. God elects to employ human lips to bring the wonder of God's word to human hearts. It is an incarnational mystery of sorts that the wonder of the Word-made-flesh is echoed in human speech. It is perhaps this holy calling with which you as a reader ought first to be confronted.

At the same time, always remember that it is finally the action of the Spirit that makes the miracle of the voiced word a reality. It is as true now as it has ever and always been that "men and women moved by the Holy Spirit spoke from God" (2 Peter 1:21). Whether the word is being brought to written form or to speech, it is the Spirit who does the moving. Humankind serves as the conduit.

With the daunting nature of the task before us, those wishing to offer themselves to this ministry of reading in the assembly might reasonably next ask, "What are the qualities we seek in readers?" What are the prerequisite gifts?

The first requirement is a "Send me! Send me!" passion for the proclaiming of the word. Where such passion is not already present in an individual, we might also look for a "would that I could" attitude: "I just don't think I can do it. I wish that I could. I would love to be able to. I am afraid I just can't." The art of reading in the assembly can be taught, but the learning process is a rigorous and continuous one.

The second requirement is perhaps a sense of humility. Among many of us who have been reading in church for a good while, there is a self-defeating and almost always deceptive self-confidence afoot that diminishes the importance of the rehearsal of readings, "because I have been doing this for years." Those who read the scripture aloud during the liturgy have been entrusted with the word in purest form beyond the bread and wine of holy communion. This responsibility begs for a little fear and trembling on the part of even the most experienced reader. One must never lose that original sense of awe and wonder at having been chosen as the spokesperson of the Divine in the hour of prayer.

God is glorified while readers and hearers are edified in our continuing commitment to reading the word as well as we possibly can. The best that we can offer can always be better.

The holy scriptures, the written and proclaimed word of God, never fail to reward those who encounter them. Those who worship in community owe their gratitude to those who give breath to that word—to you.

"Only readings that make sense make disciples.

A personal and thorough understanding of the meaning of the text paves the way for effectively sharing the text.

Listening:
The reader's first task

"Blessed rather are those who hear the word of
God and obey it!" (Luke 11:28)

Listening is the first task of those who wish to read aloud
well. Before we can *echo the joyous strain* of the word of
God, we must first hear it clearly. This takes time.

We might begin by *reading the assigned text devotionally.*
By this I mean sitting quietly with the text. Read it over
silently, perhaps several times, within the context of a
time of private prayer.

> *Listen to the words.*
> *Hear the word.*
> *Hear it as spoken directly to you.*
> *Receive the word with thanksgiving.*
> *Ponder the word prayerfully.*

Allow the text to work on you before you begin to work on the text.

It is finally impossible to help the assembly to hear what the reader has not first heard.

> This is God's word.
> This is God's work.
> Begin your preparation with prayer.

When the reader's heart, by the power of the Spirit of God, is in the right place, it is then possible to concentrate constructively on putting the word on one's lips.

Sounding out the text

Beyond how the text speaks to the reader in a devotional setting, one needs to consider the variety of sounds within every assigned text. The questions to be asked are the simple ones:

Whose voice are we hearing? Is it the voice of God; the voice of the prophet; the voice of the apostle; the voice

of Jesus; the voice of a character within the story?
Listen carefully.

How does that voice sound? Is it an angry voice; an
instructive voice; a consoling voice; a chastising voice;
a joking voice; a despairing voice; a rejoicing voice?
Listen carefully.

What are the story's details? What is happening?
What will happen? Where is the story going?
Listen carefully.

What is the prophet, the apostle, the Lord, trying to
say? Where is the text heading?
Listen carefully.

We might productively label this activity sounding out the text. When little children are stuck on a word in their early days of reading, mothers and fathers for generations have encouraged them to "sound it out." They are asking the child to discover how the arrangement of the letters ought to sound. This is a legitimate approach to any portion of the holy scripture and one that is well within the capabilities of every thoughtful person.

How one duplicates, mimics, or reproduces the text's sounds is a topic to be considered in the next section of this handbook. For the moment, the first and most critical task of the reader is to listen to the sound of the text.

It is no accident that we ask first, "How does the text sound?" rather than, "What does the text mean?" Discovering the sound of the reading will shed enormous light on its meaning. To hear the unique sounds of the text echoed on the lips of a disciplined reader will serve as oral interpretation for persons listening in worship. In many instances a text well spoken will be readily understood.

> Let the word in before
> attempting to get the word out.

That this aspect of the ministry of the lector has been often overlooked or undervalued is evident in how often the reading of one lesson has sounded much like the reading of every other. *Dusty, dry, monotonous, biblical!* are some of the adjectives that come too quickly to mind.

Certainly there will be situations in which one must do more to gain an understanding of complicated readings. The reader should never hesitate to seek clarity of understanding. Many church libraries contain a variety of tools such as commentaries, Bible dictionaries, atlases, and the like. Pastors will in almost every instance be eager to share their perspective with readers who ask.

It ought to go without saying that it is impossible to make understood texts that the reader does not understand.

"

The key to excellence
in any art form:

Practice. Practice. Practice.

Reading aloud in a public setting: 2
The basics

The object of the art of reading aloud in the assembly is to be heard and to be understood. The essential components of understandable speech are volume, pace, and enunciation. Paying attention in turn to all three will set the reader on the path to more excellent readings.

Volume

Adequate volume is our first concern. The reader's words must be heard. "Faith comes from what is heard" (Romans 10:17). Everyone in the room is entitled to hear every word. The people sitting in the last row as well as those closer to the front have all gathered, in part, for this very purpose: to hear the word. This takes some special effort on the part of the reader, especially the novice, as speaking with adequate volume to fill an entire room is not something we are often asked to do.

As a beginning focus many readers will be helped to think about reading twice as loud as they might be initially inclined. Be conscious of the distance to the last row in the room and project your voice to reach that distance. Fill the room with sound! Initially "adequate volume" will sound too loud in the reader's ears. To the ears of those relegated to the balcony, "too loud" will sound clearly audible.

> Speak up!
> Too loud is not too likely.

Microphones can help in this effort, but they can as quickly become bane as blessing. A microphone may help the reader, but it will not do the reader's work for her. It remains imperative to speak up and speak out. Avoid dropping your head when reading. "Eyes down; head up" is good advice. The words must reach the microphone before the microphone can amplify them.

Additionally, microphones come in an enormous array of types and degrees of quality. If the reader intends to use a microphone, there are several issues that need attending to in advance of the reading.

- Familiarize yourself with the microphone and its capacity (to say nothing of its idiosyncrasies) before the day of the assigned reading, while the room is empty.
- Know where and how the microphone is turned on and turned off.
- On the day of the reading, be certain in advance of the liturgy that the amplification system is in proper working order.

A mechanical note: It is not helpful to test a microphone's on and off status by tapping one's finger on the head of the microphone. These are often delicate and expensive devices. They are designed to amplify human speech, not to absorb raps and taps. One might better test the instrument's status (before the liturgy begins, of course) by saying, "Test," or—better yet—reciting a verse from scripture.

Twice as loud. Half as fast.

Pace

Appropriate pace is the reader's next concern. The words of scripture are rich with meaning. The images in the readings for the church's liturgies are many and varied. The thoughts and ideas conveyed are often complex. It takes time, even for those who are listening closely, to absorb and make sense of the words they are hearing.

As a beginning focus many readers will be helped to think about reading half as fast as they might be initially inclined. Paying close attention to each sentence's punctuation and honoring it can help enormously. Commas call for a pause. Semicolons do, as well. Colons call for a more significant pause still, while periods want to bring the reading to a stop.

Images and ideas, much like flowers, need time to bloom. Reading aloud is not unlike casting seeds. Once airborne, those seeds need time to land, settle in, and begin to germinate. The hearer needs enough time to see the image and to grasp the idea.

There is no hurry in the assembly. The proclamation of the word of God is of the essence of our gathering. It is to hear the word that people have, in large part, come. Give them enough time.

As many readings in the assembly suffer from being read too rapidly as too softly. Either error on the part of the reader will quickly discourage even those with a high level of interest and the best intentions. Human beings quickly lose interest in (and stop listening to) words they cannot hear or sentences they cannot understand.

While "half as fast" may initially strike the reader as painfully slow, faithful listeners will hear it as "utterly understandable."

> Enunciate.
> If they cannot understand it,
> they will not believe it.

Enunciation

Finally, careful enunciation must always be a critical concern. Words spoken loudly and slowly remain meaningless unless spoken crisply. Excellence in enunciation requires careful attention to consonants, especially those at the beginning and end of words. Readers who give particular attention to initial and ending *b*'s, *d*'s, *t*'s, *p*'s, *k*'s, and *s*'s will be far more readily understood than those who do not. Interior consonants (the double *t* in *little*, for example) require special attention as well when clarity of speech is the goal.

"Punching" initial consonants and "clipping" ending ones helps to give audible shape to words that are being heard and not read. Emphasizing interior consonants does the same. Clearly enunciating requires using one's lips, teeth, and tongue in carefully forming each word. Lip laziness leads to mushy speech and is the death knell to understanding.

Realizing the desire to provide members of the assembly with the unique joy of hearing the word rather than just reading along is utterly dependent on disciplined enunciation. If we hope to wean the assembly from its dependence on duplications of the texts inserted in the Sunday worship folder, crisp speech is essential.

While the "punching" and "clipping" of consonants may initially strike the reader as exaggerated or artificial, those longing to hear the word will sense it only as clear speech.

Volume, pace, and enunciation are the critical components of understandable speech. Be attentive to all three all the time and better readings will inevitably result.

Effective reading in the assembly is not merely an intellectual exercise. It is equally a physical exercise. The critical nature of volume, pace, and enunciation speak to that truth. While the art form profits from careful thinking, it requires physical practice as well. Reading aloud repeatedly in preparation is an essential prerequisite for reading aloud well for the assembly.

A proposed framework for such preparation might look like this:

1. Read the text silently—devotionally, prayerfully.
Listen carefully. Allow the text to speak to you.

2. Read the text aloud—inquisitively.
Think of it as test-driving the text. Take it out for a spin. Be attentive to the sounds you may not have heard while reading it silently. Look for trouble spots: unfamiliar words, names, and difficult phrases. Discover the meaning and pronunciation of words that are new to you and ferret out the logic or direction of difficult phrases.

3. Read the text aloud—intentionally.

Read it as though reading for the assembly. (Twice as loud, half as fast as initially inclined.) Explore the possibilities the reading presents for variation in volume and pace. Discover the various voices in the reading. Often there is more than one. Experiment with differentiating one from the other by varying volume or pace. Discover the various tones in the reading. Some readings begin with a warning or criticism and end on a more conciliatory note. Criticism should not sound the same as comfort. Warning should not sound the same as rejoicing.

4. Read the text aloud—repeatedly.

The more familiar the reader is with the text, the more assured the delivery. Discovering the pronunciation and meaning of unfamiliar words is essential. Until that new word comes trippingly off the tongue as though one had known it all along, the word is not ready for reading in the assembly. Familiarity breeds excellence!

Time is of the essence. Praying the text; pondering the text; examining and exploring the text; and practicing the text again and again take time. Until we are committed to investing that time in preparing to give voice to the word of God for the people of God, what the assembly hears will be less than it could be. A thousand occasions for joy, comfort, instruction, and the resurrection of hope will be lost forever.

" The well-prepared reader will hear the word repeatedly in the days of preparation. The assembly has but one chance.

Maximize it.

Beyond sound:
What does an excellent reading look like?

What does an excellent reading look like? This is a complex question that is too often ignored, and ignoring the question can ruin a reading before it begins.

Readers are not only heard but seen. What the assembly sees can dramatically affect what the assembly hears.

To begin, consider the source. Where does the reading come from? The holy scripture of God is the source of all the readings to which we are giving our attention. God's word is of ultimate significance in human life. If a reading is to sound significant, the visual source of the reading must look significant. Such significance is achieved in part by reading from a book of substantial size and elegance. Such significance is achieved by reading always and only from such a book. Readers should at all costs avoid reading from a bulletin insert or printed worship folder. Every reader should be sufficiently prepared so as to have no need to take the insert or worship folder itself to the reading desk at all. In a throw-away society, inserts speak of impermanence and insignificance.

Are you ready?

Significant readings look like the reader knows *where* she or he is and *what* she or he is doing. Familiarity with the layout of the text in the book from which it will be read to the assembly is essential. Is the format from which the text will be read in paragraphs or sense lines? Are the beginning and ending of the reading adequately marked in the book? Readers should arrive at the place of prayer well enough in advance of the beginning of the liturgy to have the opportunity to look at the book again and to be certain that everything at the reading desk is in readiness. Arriving early will also allow the reader time to prepare with prayer for this holy moment.

Another overarching goal of our increased preparation for reading is to pull the assembly's eyes from the printed text and to draw them to the reader or to some helpful symbol or icon in the church. It simply cannot be over-stated that we can *read* the scripture anytime and in any place. Church is one of the few places in which we are privileged to *hear* the word proclaimed. Striving for excellence in our reading is one way in which we can help the people of God make the most of this rare and precious opportunity.

The approach

Further consideration of the appearance of a reading elicits the observation that the reading does not begin when the reader opens his or her mouth. Those truly well prepared will understand that the reading begins when the reader stands up at her place in the assembly and begins the approach to the reading desk. The reader's carriage speaks volumes. One ought to approach the reading desk with purpose but without haste. We ought to be neither too casual nor too rigid. *Careful* and *prayerful* might serve us best as instructive adjectives in the physical approach to the ministry at hand.

Hands and feet

Once at the location of the reading, the issue of what to do with one's hands and one's feet deserves attention. The hands may helpfully steady the anxious reader when used to grip lightly the sides of the reading desk. Used in this way they encourage the reader to stand tall and to assert the text by taking command of both the room and the reading. In the alternative, hands resting at the reader's sides speak of self-confidence. A reader at ease puts the assembly at ease. Clasping one's hands below the waist suggests uncertainty at best, and when clasped in back, an inappropriately casual approach at worst.

While few in the assembly are likely to have the reader's feet in view, some will. Flat-on-the-floor and side-by-side is the best possible stance, providing as it does the best platform from which to project one's voice and the text's substance. Feet that are crossed betray an anxiety that the assembly can feel or, once again, suggest an inappropriately casual approach.

The face of the reading

Just as critical words do not sound the same as words of comfort, neither do they look the same. Anger has a distinct look as well as a distinct sound. So does encouragement. The physical demeanor of the reader can go a very long way indeed in underscoring the sound of the reading. To read the words "Rejoice in the Lord always; again I will say, Rejoice," with a somber face or an expressionless face is jarringly incongruent for those who are looking as well as listening. To read "You brood of vipers" with a smile can be similarly disconcerting. Once you have determined the sounds of the reading, you will do well to spend some time considering the appropriate face of the reading.

The return

As in baseball the reader's task "ain't over 'til it's over." It does not end with the conclusion of the text. Nor does it end with the announcement of the conclusion of the text. Because every reading has a look as well as a sound, it is not over until the reader is out of sight, having returned to and assumed the seat from which the reader came. Again the general rule "careful and prayerful" applies to returning to one's seat.

“

Every excellent reading
comes not only from the lips—
not only from the head—
but from the heart as well.

Put your heart into it.

Urgency:
The key to every excellent reading

"Because you are lukewarm, and neither cold
nor hot, I am about to spit you out of my mouth."
(Revelation 3:16)

"Those who fear the Lord will not be timid, or play
the coward, for he is their hope." (Sirach 34:16)

The scripture is critical of timidity in the people of God. The role of reader demands the best efforts of mighty men and women of valor.

Passion for the task and passion for the text are essential ingredients in an excellent reading. A reader can only help the hearer to feel what the reader has felt and is feeling.

> A sense of intensity is essential in holding the attention of the hearer. If the reader cares intensely, the hearer will as well.

A variety of conditions and traditions combine to diminish the boldness of the reading of scripture within the assembly. Among them, our natural anxiety about reading aloud to a crowd can easily cow the voice of the most well-intentioned. Professional performers frequently speak about the butterflies in their stomach and their continuing anxiety before going onstage. In nearly every instance their advice to others who perform in public is the same: Make the anxiety work for you. By this they mean that a certain amount of fear is to be expected and that to harness that fear by investing it in the creation of a sense of urgency can often help to bring life and vitality to the reading of the text.

The act of churchgoing in many faith traditions has an air of reserve about it. We enter quietly. We sit quietly. We may even sing quietly much of the time. A bolder, bigger reading of the word of God is in some circles a rather dramatic breaking from that tradition of reverential reserve. While it might helpfully be repeated that our desire is not to overlay the reading with artificial drama, we honor the scripture and the assembly if we mine, discover, and utilize the dramatic components inherent in the assigned text—and share them!

> There is seldom only one right
> way to read a particular text,
> but there are several wrong ways:
> Unprepared. Uninspired. Unenthused.

Intensity and urgency are not characteristics most readers bring to the table initially. We need to be encouraged to explore and develop these skills in honing the craft of reading for the assembly. Remember that it is God's law and God's gospel that are being proclaimed in every word we utter from the reading desk. These words, this moment, are matters of life and death for those who have ears. It calls for readers with brave hearts and an increasing realization of the urgency of the task at hand.

Casual doesn't cut it

Like it or not, we are living in an increasingly casual society. Seldom does one see people dressing for dinner or for the theater anymore. We are more likely to see blue jeans and shorts in worship than shirts and ties these days. Casual has become a byword in every aspect of our lives. In this vital ministry of reading, however, casual doesn't cut it. Ever. An offhanded approach to the task translates as disinterest at best and disbelief at worst. The reader must be armed to the teeth with the best of intention in preparation and a palpable sense of urgency in proclamation.

Be careful to "finish" every sentence. Do not allow your voice to trail off at the end of phrases.

Finish each statement with the energy and commitment with which it began.

Help the assembly hear every word.

Related 5 questions
and final thoughts

Over the years in workshops and discussion groups, questions have been raised by those working at this ministry that did not fit easily within the limited outline of this little handbook. Some of those questions are addressed here in case they are your own.

Should I memorize the text?

Opinions on this topic vary. Some suggest that a memorized text draws too much attention to the reader. ("Elizabeth! Can you believe he memorized that whole thing!") Others suggest that memorization of the text is the natural by-product of adequate practice—it simply happens. Certainly the less one needs to rely on the printed page, the freer one will be in the proclaiming of the word. That, it seems to me, can only benefit the assembly. Memorizing is a time-consuming proposition and until we have the text down exactly (as one would if asked to repeat the Lord's Prayer), the memorized text is not ready for delivery. Why not try it once with a shorter text? See how the hearers respond.

Should I look at the people?

This is another question on which opinions vary widely. Some again argue that such direct eye contact draws inappropriate attention to the reader. Others respond as one might expect: "I felt as though the Lord were speaking directly to me." In some circles the widely accepted practice is to urge the reader to "see the scene unfolding" just over the heads of the assembly. Most readers, most of the time, will need to keep a close eye on the written text if they hope for a smooth and coherent delivery. As stated previously, "Eyes down (on the written text), head up" is often the best rule.

What do I do if I sneeze, or cough, or lose my place?

Pause. Regroup. Go on. You may need to begin the previous sentence or phrase again. Never say, "Excuse me." Never ever apologize. The assembly knows you wish it hadn't happened. Apologizing redirects the hearer's attention to the reader and away from the reading. The reading in this moment is of the utmost importance.

Which words do I emphasize?

The simplest answer is to emphasize the words that help convey the meaning of the sentence or text being read. More often than not the emphasis moves toward the noun or the verb or the adjective rather than the pronoun. For example, Psalm 19:14:

> Wrong Way: "Let the words of **my** mouth and the meditation of **my** heart be acceptable to **you**, O LORD, my rock and my redeemer."

> Right Way: "Let the **words** of my mouth and the **meditation** of my heart be **acceptable** to you, O LORD, my rock and my redeemer."

What significance do you make of the announcement of the text?

You will want to make something of it, certainly. The announcement not only introduces the text ("A reading from Jude"); it also introduces the reader. Stand up. Speak out. Take charge. Establish your confidence and your authority at the outset. Then separate the announcement from the beginning of the reading with a significant pause. (Significant means a very deep breath; a slow three count.) The announcement signals to the assembly that this reading is an event; it is alive with God; it is proclamation. The reader is saying, "Hey! Pay attention. God has something to say to you, and it is important."

How does an excellent reading end?

At the conclusion of the reading, provide a significant pause between the end of the reading and the declaration of its having ended. Declarations such as "The word of the Lord" or "Word of God, word of life" are bold statements of faith. They ought to be delivered loudly and clearly.

And finally . . .

Reading in the assembly is of central importance for the prayer life of the church. "So faith comes from what is heard" we are reminded in Romans 10:17. Sharing that task with all who are present in the assembly represents a major advance in the liturgical life of the people of God in recent decades. Yet in many congregations we have become dangerously inattentive to the complexity of the task and sadly complacent in our preparing to accomplish it.

In general our whole approach to reading in the assembly needs to be more vigorous from beginning to end. We must recapture a sense of the honor attached to being bearers of the word, a sense of humility in the face of the challenges it presents, and a sense of joy and urgency in attending to it.

Martin Luther said that the holy scripture is the cradle in which we will find the Lord Jesus. As you prepare to read for the assembly and as you deliver the gift of the word, bear it in mind.

Bear down.

Birth the word.

Ten adverbial encouragements

Read loudly:
Fill the room with sound.

Read slowly:
Allow concepts and images time to develop in the head of the hearer.

Read distinctly:
Clip the consonants.

Read meaningfully:
Know what the text says before attempting to share the thought.

Read energetically:
Enthusiasm for the word is contagious.

Read gladly:
This is happy work.

Read reverently:
This is holy work.

Read intentionally:
"Sustain the weary with a word."

Read congruently:
Allow the body to echo the vocalized text.

Read urgently:
This work is a matter of life and death.

A few cautions

If ever they publish a reader's Bible, there are several spots at which I would urge the placement of big yellow caution signs. While the texts assigned for reading in the assembly are always loaded with possibility, not a few are fraught with potential pitfalls. Here are a few.

Revelation
Not "Revelations."
The last book of the Bible is singular. If the reader hasn't noticed, most hearers will be wondering from the outset what else the reader might have missed.

prophesy/prophecy
(See Ezekiel 37:4)
The first is a verb (action word); the second a noun (person, place, or thing), and they are pronounced differently. The assembly will suspect that the reader who offers the noun where the verb should be hasn't adequately prepared. The assembly will probably be right.

Beware Acts 2:9-10

and the names of nearly every other country and town in the ancient world (with the possible exception of Bethlehem). They are not often familiar and the reader caught unprepared will stumble badly.

Candace

(Acts 8:27)

It's an office, not a name. Ms. Bergen spells it differently.

Abel-meholah, Melchizedek, and King Ahasuerus

and the proper names of more Bible folk than you can count require special attention. Assuming that "nobody out there knows either" underestimates the intelligence of the assembly and (worse still) diminishes the importance of reading the word rightly.

" Mispronunciation
will bring the
best reading to a
screeching halt.

Suddenly the attention of the
assembly is on the reader
and no longer the word.

Pronunciation guide

The following pronunciation helps bear no official stamp. They are an attempt to render difficult words (mostly from Hebrew or Greek origin) into American-inflected English (thus *eye*-ZAY-*uh* rather than the British *eye*-ZY-*uh*).

Most sounds are presented in a consistent manner—a long *a* is pronounced *ay*; a long *o* is *oh*, and so forth. The long *i* sound is most often shown with a *y*, but where it stands alone, it is represented by *eye*, and as a way of differentiating the noun *prophecy* from the verb *prophesy*, the long *i* at the end of the latter is designated PROF-*uh-sy*.

Note that an *h* at the end of a syllable relates only to the vowel preceding it, and should not be voiced. Thus, in *sheh*-OHL, the second *h* is intended only to show a short *e* sound.

Some of the pronunciations may seem obvious; the intent is to be relatively comprehensive. Pronunciations may, of

course, be altered from these suggestions if another us-
age is preferred.

A

Abana = uh-BAN-uh
Abba = AH-buh
Abednego = uh-BED-nih-go
Abel-meholah = ay-bul-muh-HO-luh
Abiathar = uh-BY-uh-thar
Abilene = ab-ih-LEE-neh
Abinadab = uh-BIN-uh-dab
Abinoam = uh-BIH-no-um
Abishai = uh-BY-shy
Abram = AY-brum
Absalom = AB-suh-lum
Achaia = uh-KAY-uh
Achor = AY-kor
Adar = AY-dar
Admah = AD-muh
Agabus = AH-guh-bus
Ahasuerus = uh-hazh-oo-ER-us
Ahaz = AY-haz
Ahio = uh-HI-oh
Ai = eye
Alphaeus = al-FEE-us

Amalekites = AM-uh-leh-kytz
Amaziah = am-uh-ZY-uh
Amittai = uh-MIT-eye
Ammonites = AM-uh-nytz
Amorites = AM-uh-rytz
Amoz = AY-moz
Ananias = an-uh-NY-us
Apphia = AP-fee-uh
Arabah = AIR-uh-buh
Aram = EHR-um
Aramean = ehr-uh-MEE-un
Arameans = ehr-uh-MEE-unz
Archippus = ar-KIP-us
Areopagus = ar-ih-OP-uh-gus
Arimathea = ar-ih-muh-THEE-uh
Ashkelon = ASH-kel-un
Assyria = uh-SIH-ree-uh
Athenians = uh-THEEN-ee-unz
Augustus = aw-GUS-tus
Azotus = ah-ZOH-tus

B

Baal = BAY-ul
Baal-shalishah = bay-ul-SHAL-uh-shuh
Baale-judah = bay-ul-ih-JOO-duh

Baals = BAY-ulz
Babel = BAY-bul
Babylon = BAB-ih-lon
Barabbas = buh-RAB-us
Barachiah = bar-uh-KY-uh
Barak = BAR-uk
Barsabbas = bar-SAB-us
Bartimaeus = bar-tim-AY-us
Baruch = buh-ROOK
Bathsheba = bath-SHE-buh
Beelzebul = bee-EL-zeh-bul
Beer-lahai-roi = beer-luh-HI-roy
Beer-sheba = beer-SHE-buh
Belshazzar = bel-SHAZ-ur
Beth-peor = beth-PEE-or
Beth-zatha = beth-ZAY-thuh
Bethlehemite = BETH-leh-myt
Bethphage = BETH-fuh-juh
Bethsaida = beth-SAY-uh-duh
Bethuel = beh-THOO-el
Bilhah = BILL-hah
bitumen = buh-TYOO-mun
Boaz = BOH-az

C

Caesarea Philippi = sez-uh-REE-uh fil-IP-eye
Caiaphas = KAY-uh-fus
Cana = KAY-nuh
Canaan = KAY-nun
Canaanite = KAY-nuh-nyt
Canaanites = KAY-nuh-nytz
Cananaean = kay-nuh-NEE-un
Candace = KAN-duh-suh
Capernaum = kuh-PER-nuh-um
Cappadocia = kap-uh-DOH-shee-uh
Carmel = CAR-mel
centurion = sen-CHUR-ee-un
Cephas = SEE-fus
Chaldeans = kahl-DEE-unz
Chilion = KIL-ih-un
Chuza = KOO-zuh
Cilicia = sih-LISH-yuh
Cleopas = KLEE-uh-pus
Colossae = kuh-LOS-ee
Colossians = kuh-LOSH-unz
Crescens = CRES-enz
Cyrene = sy-REE-neh
Cyrenians = sy-REE-nee-unz
Cyrus = SY-rus

D

Dalmatia = dal-MAY-shuh
Decapolis = deh-CAP-oh-lis
Demas = DEE-mus
denarii = den-AR-ee-eye
denarius = den-AR-ee-us
Deuteronomy = dew-ter-ON-uh-mee
Diblaim = DIB-lih-um
Dothan = DOH-thun

E

Ecclesiastes = ek-lee-zee-ASS-teez
Edom = EE-dum
Ehud = EE-hud
Elah = EE-luh
Eldad = EL-dad
Eli = EE-ly
Eli, lema sabachthani = EL-ee, LEM-uh suh-BAHK-
  thun-ee
Eliab = eh-LY-ub
Eliam = eh-LY-um
Eliezer = el-ih-EE-zer
Elimelech = eh-LIM-eh-lek
Elkanah = el-KAY-nuh

Eloi, lema sabachthani = EL-oh-ee, LEM-uh suh-
  BAHK-thun-ee
Epaphras = EP-uh-frus
ephah = EE-fuh
Ephesians = eh-FEE-zhunz
Ephesus = EF-uh-sus
ephod = EE-fod
Ephphatha = EF-uh-thuh
Ephraim = EF-rum
Ephrathah = EF-ruh-thuh
Ephrathites = EF-ruh-thytz
Euodia = you-OH-dee-uh
Euphrates = you-FRAY-teez
Ezekiel = eh-ZEE-kee-el

G

Gabbatha = GAB-uh-thuh
Galatia = guh-LAY-shuh
Galatians = guh-LAY-shunz
Gennesaret = geh-NES-uh-rut
Gerasenes = GEHR-uh-seenz
Gethsemane = geth-SEM-uh-nee
Gibeah = GIB-ee-uh
Gibeon = GIB-ee-un
Gilboa = gil-BOH-uh

Gilead = GIL-ee-ad
Gilgal = GIL-gol
Gomer = GO-mer
Gomorrah = guh-MOR-uh
Goshen = GOH-shun

H

Habakkuk = huh-BAK-uk
Hades = HAY-deez
Hagar = HAY-gar
Haggai = HAG-eye
Hakeldama = huh-KEL-duh-muh
Haman = HAY-mun
Hanamel = HAN-uh-mel
Hananiah = han-uh-NY-uh
Haran = HAR-un
Harosheth-ha-goiim = huh-RO-sheth-huh-GOY-im
Hazael = HAY-zuh-el
Hazor = HAY-zor
Hebron = HE-brun
heifer = HEF-er
hemorrhages = HEM-or-uh-juhz
Herodians = heh-ROH-dee-unz
Herodias = heh-ROH-dee-us
Hezekiah = hez-eh-KY-uh

Hivites = HIH-vytz
Horeb = HO-reb
Hosea = ho-ZAY-uh
hypocrisy = hih-POK-ris-ee
hypocrites = HIP-uh-crits
hyssop = HISS-up

I

idolaters = eye-DOL-uh-terz
impiety = im-PY-uh-tee
iniquities = ih-NIK-wit-eez
Isaiah = eye-ZAY-uh
Iscariot = is-CAR-ee-ut
Ishmaelites = ISH-muh-lytz
Israelites = IS-rul-eytz
Ittai = IT-eye
Ituraea = it-uh-REE-uh

J

Jabbok = JAB-uk
Jabin = JAY-bin
Japheth = JAY-fith
Jashar = JAY-shur
Jebusites = JEB-you-sytz

Jehoiada = juh-HOY-uh-duh
Jehoiakim = jeh-HOY-uh-kim
Jehozadak = jeh-HOZE-uh-dak
Jehu = JEE-hoo
Jemimah = jeh-MY-muh
Jephthah = JEF-thuh
Jeremiah = jehr-uh-MY-uh
Jericho = JEHR-ih-koh
Jeroboam = jehr-uh-BO-um
Jezreel = JEZ-re-ul
Jezreelite = JEZ-re-uh-lyt
Joab = JOH-ab
Joash = JOH-ash
Job = JOHB
Joses = JOH-sis
Josiah = joh-SY-uh
Jotham = JOH-thum

K

Kedar = KEE-dur
Kedesh = KEE-desh
Keren-happuch = ker-en HAP-uk
Keziah = keh-ZY-uh

L

Laban = LAY-bun
Lappidoth = LAP-uh-doth
Lazarus = LAZ-uh-rus
Levi = LEE-vy
Levites = LEE-vytz
Leviticus = leh-VIT-ih-cus
licentiousness = ly-SEN-chus-ness
Lo-ammi = lo-AM-eye
Lo-ruhamah = lo-roo-HAY-muh
Lucius = LOO-shus
Lydda = LID-uh
Lydia = LID-ee-uh
Lysanias = lih-SAY-nee-us

M

Macedonia = mass-uh-DOHN-ee-uh
Mahlon = MAH-lun
Mahseiah = mah-SEE-uh
Malachi = MAL-uh-ky
Malchus = MAL-kus
Mamre = MAM-rih
Manaen = MAN-ih-en
Manasseh = muh-NAS-uh

Massah = MAS-uh
Matthias = muh-THY-us
Medad = MEE-dad
Melchizedek = mel-KIZ-uh-dek
Meribah = MEH-rih-bah
Meshach = ME-shak
Mesopotamia = mes-oh-poh-TAY-mee-uh
Micah = MY-kuh
Michal = MY-kul
Midian = MID-ee-un
Midianite = MID-ee-uh-nyt
Moab = MO-ab
Mordecai = MOR-deh-ky
Moreh = MOR-eh
Moriah = moh-RY-uh

N

Naaman = NAY-uh-mun
Naboth = NAY-bahth
Nahor = NAY-hor
Naphtali = NAF-tuh-lye
nazirite = NAZ-uh-ryt
Neapolis = nee-AP-uh-lis
Nebo = NEE-boh
Nebuchadnezzar = neb-uh-kud-NEZ-ur

Nebuchadrezzar = neh-buh-kud-REZ-ur
Negeb = NEG-eb
Nehemiah = nee-eh-MY-uh
Neriah = neh-RY-uh
Nicodemus = nick-uh-DEEM-us
Niger = NY-ger
Nimshi = NIM-shee
Nineveh = NIN-uh-vuh

O

Obed = OH-bed
Obed-edom = oh-bed-EE-dum
oblation = oh-BLAY-shun
Onesimus = oh-NES-ih-mus

P

Paddan-aram = pad-un-AR-um
Pamphylia = pam-FIL-yuh
Paphos = PA-fus
Paran = PAR-un
Peniel = peh-NY-el
Peninnah = peh-NIN-uh
Penuel = peh-NOO-el
Perizzites = PEH-rih-zytz

perseverance = per-seh-VEAR-untz
Phanuel = FAN-oo-el
Pharaoh = FAIR-oh
Pharisee = FAIR-uh-see
Pharpar = FAR-par
Philemon = fy-LEE-mun
Philippi = fih-LIP-eye
Philippians = fih-LIP-ee-unz
Phoenicia = fuh-NEESH-yuh
Phrygia = FRIJ-yuh
phylacteries = fih-LAK-ter-eez
Pisgah = PIZ-guh
Pisidia = pih-SID-yuh
Pithom = PY-thum
porticoes = POR-tih-koz
prophecy = PROF-uh-see
prophesy = PROF-uh-sy
Puah = POO-uh

Q

Quirinius = kwih-RIN-ee-us

R

Rabbah = RAB-uh
Rabbouni = ruh-BOON-ih
Rahab = RAY-hab
Ramah = RAY-muh
Rameses = RAM-uh-seez
Rephidim = REF-uh-dim

S

Sadducees = SAD-yuh-seez
Salome = sah-LOH-mih
Samaria = suh-MAIR-ee-uh
Samaritan = suh-MAIR-it-un
Samaritans = suh-MAIR-it-unz
Samothrace = SAM-uh-thrays
Sarai = SEHR-eye
satraps = SAY-traps
Scythian = SITH-ee-un
Seba = SEE-buh
Shadrach = SHAD-rak
Shammah = SHAH-mah
Shaphat = SHAH-fut
Shealtiel = she-AL-tih-el
Sheba = SHE-buh

Shechem = SHEK-em
shekels = SHEK-ulz
Sheol = sheh-OHL
Shiloh = SHY-lo
Shinar = SHY-nar
Shiphrah = SHIF-ruh
Sidon = SY-dun
Siloam = sih-LOH-um
Silvanus = sil-VAY-nus
Simeon = SIM-ee-un
Sinai = SY-ny
Sirach = SIHR-ahk
Sisera = SIS-uh-ruh
Sychar = SY-car
Syene = sy-EE-nih
synagogue = SIN-uh-gog
synagogues = SIN-uh-gogz
Syntyche = SIN-tih-kih
Syrian = SIHR-ee-un
Syrophoenician = sy-ro-fuh-NISH-un

T

tabernacle = TAB-er-nak-ul
Tabor = TAY-bor
talitha cum = tuh-LEE-thuh KOOM

Tarshish = TAR-shish
Terah = TEH-ruh
terebinth = TEHR-eh-binth
Thaddaeus = THAD-ee-us
Theophilus = thee-OFF-il-us
Thessalonians = thes-uh-LOAN-ee-unz
Thessalonica = thes-uh-loh-NY-kuh
Thyatira = thy-uh-TY-ruh
Tiberias = ty-BIHR-ee-us
Titus = TY-tus
Trachonitis = track-uh-NY-tis
trigon = TRY-gon
Troas = TROH-us
Tyre = TYR

U

Ur = uhr
Uriah = yuh-RY-uh
Uzzah = UZ-uh
Uzziah = uh-ZY-uh

W

wadi = WAH-dee
Wadi Kishon = WAH-dee KY-shun

Z

Zacchaeus = zak-EE-us
Zarephath = ZAR-eh-fath
Zarethan = ZAIR-uh-than
Zealot = ZEL-ut
zealous = ZEL-us
Zebedee = ZEB-uh-dee
Zeboiim = zeh-boy-EEM
Zebulun = ZEB-you-lun
Zechariah = zek-uh-RY-uh
Zedekiah = zed-eh-KY-uh
Zephaniah = zef-uh-NY-uh
Zerubbabel = zeh-RUB-uh-bul
Ziklag = ZIK-lag
Zilpah = ZIL-puh
Zoar = ZOH-ur